THE LITTLE BOOK OF
Scottish Wit
and Wisdom

D0774180

THE LITTLE BOOK OF

Scottish Wit and Wisdom

BETTY KIRKPATRICK

Michael O'Mara Humour

First published in Great Britain in 2001 by
Michael O'Mara Books Limited
9 Lion Yard, Tremadoc Road
London SW4 7NQ

Copyright © Michael O'Mara Books Limited 2001

A CIP catalogue record for this book is available
from the British Library

ISBN 1-85479-826-X

1 3 5 7 9 10 8 6 4 2

Designed and typeset by Martin Bristow

Printed in Australia by McPherson's Printing Group

Contents

Introduction

SCOTLAND has had its fair share of comedians, both professional and self-styled, but the wit of Scotland is not traditionally of the ha-ha, belly-laugh variety. Rather it is of an understated, wry-smile type, known in Scotland as pawkie humour. The *Concise Scots Dictionary* defines pawkie as 'having a matter-of-fact, humorously critical outlook on life, characterized by a sly, quiet wit', which sums it up very well.

Alas this dry style of humour has the disadvantage that, unlike the obvious joke, it can go unnoticed. It is partly for this reason that Scots have acquired a reputation in some quarters of being dour or humourless, but often the fault has lain in the hearers who did not recognize wit when it was presented to them.

There is less need to explain the wisdom of the Scots, since Scotland, especially considering its size, has produced a great number of people who have made a significant contribution to the shaping of the world. These have included people from a wide range of disciplines, such as poets, philosophers, novelists, artists, architects, engineers, explorers, doctors, scientists and so on, and the thoughts of some of these are included in the following selection of sayings and quotations.

Any collection of these, especially such a short one, is bound to be extremely personal and I have decided to concentrate on the traditional and the historical. In this modern age where so much is disposable and so ephemeral, it is good, I think, to give prominence, at least occasionally, to the tried and the true.

The Scots have their own language that developed quite separately from English, although they share a common ancestor in Old English. Over the centuries, however, for various political, educational and cultural reasons, English gradually became the dominant language in Scotland, and now, though valiant efforts are being made to revive the flagging spirits of the Scots language, there are many people, especially of the younger generation, who know, at best, only a few words of it. Thus, although several of the traditional sayings in proverbs contain Scots words, these are absent from many of the quoted writers because they penned their thoughts in English.

A short glossary has been added as a guide to the Scots element in the book. In case you are puzzled over any of the spellings of Scots words, it should be remembered that Scots, unlike English and most other languages, lacks a standard spelling scheme. This inevitably gives rise to one word having several variants, making it almost impossible to misspell a Scots word.

Sage Sayings & Pithy Proverbs

HEALTH

Better wear shoon than sheets.
*It is better to wear shoes to keep the feet warm
and dry (even though this may be expensive)
rather than become ill.*

A cauld needs the cook as muckle
as the doctor.
*Nutritious food can cure a cold as effectively
as medicine.*

Feed a cauld and starve a fever.

Traditional advice about giving nutritious food to people suffering with a cold is not always appropriate if they have a fever.

Feed a cauld but hunger a colic.
A similar sentiment to the previous saying,
where the condition not requiring nourishment
is a stomach disorder.

Fill fu' and haud fu' maks a stark man.
Plenty of good food and drink makes a person strong.

Gae tae bed wi' the lamb
and rise wi' the laverock.
A recipe for remaining healthy; a Scots version
of 'early to bed, early to rise'.

He that eats but ae dish seldom needs the doctor.

A warning to be sparing in the amount of food you eat, if you want to remain healthy.

If ye want to be soon weel be lang sick.

Not a recommendation to malinger, but advice not to get out of bed too soon after you have been ill.

Licht suppers mak lang days.

A recommendation to eat sparingly, especially in the evening, if you wish to live to an old age.

Rise when the day daws,
Bed when the nicht fa's.
*An injunction to stay healthy by going
to bed early and getting up early.*

Suppers kill mair than doctors cure.
*Another recommendation to eat sparingly,
especially in the evening.*

FOOD

A drap and a bit's but sma' requite.
*Said as an invitation to guests to partake of food
and drink, indicating that this is little recompense
for their friendship.*

A hungry man's
an angry man.
*This speaks for itself –
it is undoubtedly true
that many people
become bad-tempered
when they get hungry.*

A hungry man's meat is lang o' makin' ready.
*When you're very hungry the preparation of your
food seems to take a very long time; a similar
saying to 'a watched pot never boils'.*

A hungry wame has nae lugs.
*Those who are hungry seem to lose the power of
hearing and so don't listen to reason.*

A kiss and a drink o' watter mak
a wersh breakfast.
*Said as a warning to a couple who think they
can live on love and very little else.*

As the soo fills, the draff soors.

Literally, as the sow fills up, its food begins to taste sour; a compliment to a host to express that the food has been so plentiful and so good that the guest's appetite has been fully satisfied and he/she can eat no more.

Bannocks are better than nae breid.

Very plain food is better than no food at all; a similar saying to 'half a loaf is better than no bread'.

Better belly burst than gude meat spoil.
*It is better to eat too much than let good food
go to waste; said by those who eat too much,
as justification for their greed.*

Better wait on the cook than the doctor.
*A reference to the fact that many people felt that
the ill would benefit more from nourishing food
than medicine, although this could vary
with the type of illness.*

Breid's hoose is skailed never.
*If a house contains bread you can never say
it has no food in it.*

Eat in measure and defy the doctor.
Moderation in eating makes for a healthy life.

Eats meat, an's never fed; wears claes
and never cled.
*No matter how well-fed or well-clothed some people
may be, they never seem to look any better for it.*

Eat weel's drink weel's brither.
Eating well and drinking well should go together.

Fat paunches bode lean pows.
People who are greedy and over-fed have empty heads.

Hunger's good kitchen.
When you're hungry any food tastes good.

Hunger's good kitchen to a cauld potato, but
a wet divot to the lowe o' love.
*Hunger makes the humblest of food (such as a cold
potato) seem very appetizing, but it dampens
down romantic passion.*

I'm neither sma' drink thirsty
nor grey bread hungry.
*Said by someone who is disappointed at the standard
of fare that he/she has been offered by a host.*

Mennans are better than nae meat.
*Both this and the saying overleaf indicate that it is
better to have very little food than no food at all. In
Scots the word meat is often used for food in general
and mennans are minnows or very small fish.*

Poor folk seek meat for their stamacks and
rich folk seek stamacks for their meat.
*The poor eat because they're hungry, the rich because
they feel they have to, even if they have little appetite.*

Mennans are better than nae fish.
See the saying on the previous page.

Naething sooner maks a man auld-like
than fitting ill to his meat.
Nothing ages people so rapidly as being ill-fed.

Ne'er gie' me death in a toom dish.
A jocular saying used by people who like their food and
want some of it, literally meaning 'don't give me death
by means of an empty dish, don't starve me to death'.

Ne'er speak ill o' them whose breid ye eat.
A warning not to criticize your host.

O' a' the meat in the warld,
the drink gaes best doon.
This speaks for itself in a land
that makes and loves whisky.

Some hae meat and canna eat
And some wad meat that want it;
But we hae meat and we can eat,
For which the Lord be thankit.
A grace said before meals, known as the Selkirk Grace.

They may ken by your beard what has been
on your board.
A way of telling someone that some of the food he has
just eaten is stuck on his beard or chin.

The nearer the grave, the greedier.
The older people get, the more food they like to have.

Stuffin' hauds oot storms.
*Advice given to people who are setting out on a
journey in bad weather to eat well before they leave.*

Welcome's the best dish in the kitchen.
Food given with a good will tastes the best.

They hae need o'a canny cook that hae
but ae egg to their denner.
*It takes a clever, ingenious cook to make a meal out of
very little; also extended to mean that it takes a
resourceful person to make the most of what is to hand.*

Tak a piece – your teeth's longer
than your beard.
*Words of encouragement said to children to get them to
take a titbit or treat when they have the chance.*

Ye hae tint your ain stamack
an' found a tyke's.
*A remark made to someone who is eating
a great deal as though very hungry.*

Your meat will mak you bonny
and when you're bonny you'll be well lo'ed
and when you're well lo'ed you'll be
licht-hearted and when you're licht-hearted
you'll loup far.
Said to children to encourage them to eat.

What's in your wame's no in your testament.
Said as an encouragement to someone to eat up;
a reminder that if you eat everything on your plate
you cannot leave it to someone else in your will.

When all fruit fa's, welcome ha's.
When we have consumed all the finer food, we must
be content with the plain kind.

WEATHER

About the moon there is a brough,
The weather will be cold and rough.
*A warning of rough weather if there is a halo effect
round the moon.*

A green Yule maks a fat kirkyard.
*A wet winter results in many deaths
because of the many illnesses that are caused
or worsened by damp conditions.*

As the day lengthens, the cauld strengthens.

A reminder that when the days begin to get longer, the weather often becomes colder.

Cast not a clout till May be oot.

Often taken to mean that people should not remove any of their winter clothing until the month of May has passed. However, it is thought by some that May refers to the hawthorn, the advice being not to remove any winter clothes until the hawthorn is in blossom.

East and wast the sign o' a blast; north
and south, the sign o' a drouth.
*A saying that uses the direction of
the prevailing wind to forecast the weather.*

E'ening grey an' a morning red,
put on your hat or ye'll
wet your head.
E'ening red an' a morning
grey, is a taiken o' a
bonny day.
*A weather saying with a
similar meaning to 'red sky
at night, shepherd's delight,
red sky in the morning, shepherd's
warning'.*

If Candlemas Day be dry and fair
The hauf o' winter's to come and mair.
If Candlemas Day be wet and foul,
The hauf o' winter's gaun at Yule.
*Candlemas Day is February 2 and it was taken as
a good weather sign if it was wet on that day.*

If grass grows green in Janaveer,
It will be the waur for it a' the year.
*The belief was that if the grass was green too early in
the year, it was unlikely to survive the rest of the year.*

Mony haws, mony snaws.
*A warning that a good harvest of haw berries
will result in a cold, hard winter.*

Mist in May and heat in June make the
harvest right soon.

A self-evident weather saying.

Sorrow an' ill weather come unca'd.

Both ill fortune and ill weather are beyond our control.

The rain cams scouth, when the wind's
i' the south.

*In this context scouth means freely, without restraint,
and so the saying indicates that heavy rain will occur
when there a wind blowing from the south.*

When the moon is on her back
Gae mend your shoon and sort your thack.

*When the moon appears in such a position,
it should be seen as a sign of rain, and appropriate
measures should be taken.*

Under water dearth, under snaw bread.

*A field that has been flooded with water will produce
a very poor crop, but one that has been covered
in snow will produce a good one.*

MONEY

A' complain o' want o' siller,
but nane o' want o' sense.
*A saying indicating that desiring more money
is a far more common human preoccupation
than desiring more sense.*

A deaf man will hear the clink o' money.
A saying that emphasizes the lure of money very well.

Get what you can, and keep what you hae,
that's the way to get rich.
*It sounds so easy that it makes you wonder why
there are not more rich people around!*

A fu' sack can bear a clout i' the side.
*A prosperous person can afford to take a few knocks
from fate.*

Better a tocher in her than wi' her.
*A tocher was a woman's dowry and this saying
suggests that it was better for a woman to have
good qualities within, rather than have a lot
of money and possessions.*

Gathering gear
is weel-liket wark.
*Acquiring money is
generally thought
to be a pleasant
occupation.*

He's got his nose in a gude kail pat.
Literally, he has got his head in a good soup pot;
said of a person who has married someone well-off.

He wad rake hell for a bodle.
A saying indicating how much someone loves money
and what a miser he is, a bodle being an old
copper coin.

Eaten meat is ill to pay.
No one likes to have to pay for something
that has already been consumed.

Lay your wame to your winning.
A warning not to consume more than you earn.

It's folly to live poor to dee rich.
The moral is self-evident, akin to
'you can't take it with you'.

Moyen does muckle, but moyen does mair.
Influence can do a lot, but money is even more
powerful.

There are nane sae weel shod but may slip.
Everyone, including the wealthy, is at risk from
misfortune and mishaps.

He wad skin a louse for the tallow.
A saying that describes just how miserly someone is.

It's as easy to get siller frae a lawyer
as butter frae a black dog's hause.
*Hause means throat in this instance, so
the saying suggests that acquiring silver
from a lawyer is an impossible feat.*

Wealth gars wits waver.
*People tend to lose their common sense
when money is involved.*

Wealth has made mair men covetous than
covetousness has made men wealthy.
A warning against greed.

The siller penny slays mair souls
than the nakit sword slays bodies.
A comment on the destructive power of money.

Put twa pennies in a purse
and they will creep thigither.
*A saying indicating how money
soon accumulates if you save it.*

Want o' wit is waur than want o' gear.
*It is worse to be lacking in intelligence
and sense than to be lacking in money.*

SILENCE

A close mou catches nae flees.

A recommendation to say as little as possible; a variation on 'shut your mouth and you'll get no flies'.

Ah dinna bile ma cabbages twice.

Said as a refusal to repeat what has just been said; literally 'I don't boil my cabbages twice'.

Dinna open yer mou tae fill ither fowks.
A warning not to gossip.

Gie yer tongue mair holidays than yer heid.
*An imaginative way of suggesting that people
should think more than they speak.*

Keep yer mou shut and yer een open.
*A warning that you will learn more if you say little
and observe a lot.*

Keep your breath tae cool yer parritch.
*A piece of advice given to someone who is
wasting words.*

[41]

He that spares to speak, spares to speed.
*A saying not in favour of silence, but one that suggests
that people who don't point out their own talents
don't succeed.*

Keep yer gab steekit
when ye kenna yer company.
*A warning not to say too much in front of strangers;
literally to keep your mouth closed when you don't
know who is present.*

Put your thoom on that!
*Literally, put your thumb on that; said as
a warning to keep something secret.*

Pint stoups
hae lang lugs.
*A reminder
that those
who drink
too much
often say too much.*

The loodest bummer's no the best bee.
*The person who says the most is rarely
the most effective person.*

When a' men speak, nae man hears.
*If everyone speaks at once, no one hears or takes in
anything that is said.*

Think mair than ye say.
Devote more time to thought than speech.

Wae is the wife
that wants a tongue,
but weel's the man
that gat her.
*It is unfortunate to be a
woman who says very
little, since little notice
will be taken of her,
but it is fortunate to be
a man who marries
such a woman.*

Wide lugs and a short tongue are best.
It is best to listen a lot and say very little.

TRUTH

A fu' heart never lied.
People are more likely to tell the truth
when they are in the grip of emotion.

Auld saws speak truths.
There's a lot of truth in old sayings,
as this collection proves.

Craft maun hae claes, but truth gangs nakit.
*Cunning may be disguised, but truth does not need
any cover or embellishment.*

Facts are chiels that winna ding.
Facts, and therefore the truth, cannot be denied.

He never lies, but when the holly's green.
*Since holly is an evergreen tree, this saying indicates
that the person in question never tells the truth.*

If a'thing's true, that's nae lee.
*A saying used to express disbelief
in what has just been said.*

It's a sin to lee on the diel.
You should always speak the truth,
even where wicked people are concerned.

Truth and honesty keep the croon
on the causey.
People who are honest and truthful stay out
of trouble. The 'croon o' the causey' or the crown
of the causeway was the highest part of the street,
farthest way from the gutter where all the
rubbish gathered.

Truth will stand when a'thing's failin'.
Truth can be relied upon when everything else fails.

WORDS

A' are no freens that speak us fair.
*Just because someone pays you a compliment
or says something nice about you, you cannot
assume that he/she is your friend.*

A' his buzz shaks nae barley.
*Said of someone who may say a great deal but
whose words have no effect on the situation.*

A man o' words but no' o' deeds
is like a garden fu' o' weeds.
*A saying telling us that actions
are much more useful than mere words.*

Bairns speak i' the field whit
they hear i' the ha'.
*A warning to parents to be careful
what they say in front of their
children in case what was uttered in
private is repeated in public.*

Muckle spoken, part spilt.
*Said of a subject which has been
talked about to such an extent
that much of its meaning has
been lost or ignored.*

Praise without profit puts little i' the pat.
Fine words alone are not much practical use to anyone.

Glib i' the tongue is aye glaikit at the heart.
*Another saying that warns against being impressed
or taken in by the flattery of smooth-talking people,
as they are very likely to be insincere.*

Words are but wind,
but dunts are the devil.
Physical blows are much worse than verbal abuse.

Fair words winna mak
the pot boil.
*A saying that stresses the
inadequacy of mere words.*

Bees that hae honey in their mouths
hae stings in their tails.

A warning to be wary of people who are particularly
eloquent or flattering, as they may be up to no good.

There's a word in my wame,
but it's o'er far down.

A saying used by someone to indicate that he/she
cannot think of the right word at that moment;
similar to having a word on the tip of your tongue.

Sticks and stanes may brak my banes,
But names will never hurt me.
*A saying indicating that, although physical abuse
may do harm to someone, verbal insults will not;
often used by schoolchildren to their tormentors.*

Thanks winna feed the cat.
*Verbal thanks is not worth much; sometimes said
as a grudging, belittling acknowledgement
of spoken thanks.*

Ye wad wheedle a
laverock frae the lift.
*Said to someone who is
particularly charming
or persuasive, as though
they are able to persuade
the lark to leave the sky.*

It's a gude tongue
that says nae ill,
but a better heart
that thinks none.
*A self-evident
saying that praises
the harbouring
of charitable thoughts.*

Quotations

John Logie Baird (1888–1946)
television pioneer

Seeing by wireless.

A definition of television ascribed to him

LADY FRANCES BALFOUR (1858–1931)
writer and suffragist

———

Golf has ceased to be a peculiarly national game. It is now no longer a pastime for the impecunious Scot, armed with two or three clubs, and a feather ball, it has become a professional sport, pursued by devastating hordes of foreigners among whom the American tongue rises shrill and strident.

Ne Obliviscaris:
Dinna Forget (1930)

J. M. BARRIE (1860–1937)
playwright and novelist

We are undoubtedly a sentimental people, and it sometimes plays havoc with that other celebrated sense of ours, the practical.

From a speech to the Royal Scottish Corporation on 30 November 1928

We cannot tell the precise moment when
friendship is formed. As in filling a vessel
drop by drop, there is at last a drop that
makes it run over; so in a series of kindnesses,
there is at last one which makes the
heart run over.

Life of Samuel Johnson (1791)

JOHN BUCHAN (1875–1940)
writer and statesman

The dominant thought of youth is the
bigness of the world, of age its smallness.
As we grow older we escape from the tyranny
of matter and recognize that the true
centre of gravity is the mind.

Memory Hold-the-Door (1941)

ROBERT BURNS (1759–96)
poet and song-writer

Princes and lords are but the breath of kings,
'An honest man's the noblest work o' God'.

The Cotter's Saturday Night (1785) – Burns quotes
Alexander Pope

The best-laid schemes o' mice and men
Gang aft agley,
An' leave us nought but grief an' pain,
For promis'd joy!

To a Mouse (1785) – oft-quoted lines commenting
on the essential fallibility of plans and hopes

Then gently scan your brother Man,
Still gentler sister woman,
Tho' they may gang a kennin' wrang,
To step aside is human.

Address to the Unco' Guid (1786) – lines
that urge people to refrain from passing
judgement on others

O wad some Power the giftie gie us
To see oursels as ithers see us!
It wad frae monie a blunder free us,
An' foolish notion.

To a Louse (1786) – a poem written when he saw
such a creature on a lady's hat in church, with lines
indicating that we would not behave so foolishly
if we could view ourselves with the eyes of others

But pleasures are like poppies spread,
You seize the flower, its bloom is shed,
   Or like the snow falls in the river,
   A moment white – then melts forever.

Tam o' Shanter (1790) – lines indicating that Burns
could be lyrical in English as well as Scots

Then let us pray that come it may,
As come it will, for a' that,
That sense and worth, o'er a' the earth'
Shall bear the gree, an a' that;
For a' that and a' that,
It's comin' yet for a' that,
That man to man the world o'er,
Shall brothers be for a' that.

For a' that and a' that (1795)

Thomas Carlyle (1795–1881)
historian and essayist

In the long run every Government is the
exact symbol of its People, with their wisdom
and their unwisdom; we have to say,
Like People like Government.

Past and Present (1843)

A well-written Life is almost as rare as a well-spent one.

Critical and Miscellaneous Essays (1838)

If Jesus Christ were to come today, people would not even crucify him. They would ask him to dinner, and hear what he had to say, and make fun of it.

Carlyle at His Zenith (1927) by D. A. Wilson

ANDREW CARNEGIE (1835–1919)
industrialist and philanthropist

There is an unwritten law among the best workmen: 'Thou shalt not take thy neighbour's job.'

Forum (August 1886)

Golf is an indispensable adjunct to high civilization.

Said when leaving a large sum of money to Yale University to build a golf course

LORD HENRY COCKBURN (1779–1854)
judge

———————

I never see a scene of Scotch beauty, without
being thankful that I have beheld it before
it has been breathed over by the angel
of mechanical destruction.

Circuit Journeys (1847)

SIR ARTHUR CONAN DOYLE (1859–1930)
novelist – creator of Sherlock Holmes

It is a capital mistake to theorize before one has data. Insensibly one begins to twist facts to suit theories, instead of theories to suit facts.

A Scandal in Bohemia (1891)

SIR ALEXANDER FLEMING (1881–1955)
bacteriologist and discoverer of penicillin

This thirst for immediate results is by
no means uncommon, but it is extremely
harmful. Really valuable research is a
long-term affair.

The Life of Sir Alexander Fleming (1959)
by André Maurois

A good gulp of whisky at bedtime – it's not
very scientific, but it helps.

A remedy for the common cold ascribed to him

SIR PATRICK GEDDES (1854–1932)
townplanner and biologist

When an idea is dead it is embalmed
in a textbook.

The Worlds of Patrick Geddes (1978)
by Philip Boardman

(James) Keir Hardie (1856–1915)
Labour politician

I think it could be shown that the position of
women, as of most other things, has always
been better, nearer to equality, with man, in
Celtic, than in non-Celtic, races.

DAVID HUME (1711–76)
philosopher and historian

The great end of all human industry is the
attainment of happiness. For this were arts
invented, science cultivated, laws ordained
and societies modelled by the most profound
wisdom of patriots and legislators.

Essays: Moral, Political and Literary,
'The Stoic' (1742)

DAVID LIVINGSTONE (1813–73)
missionary and explorer

The strangest thing I have seen in this country seems really to be broken-heartedness and it attacks free men who have been captured and made slaves.

Last Journal of David Livingstone
in Central Africa (1874)

HUGH McDIARMID, PSEUDONYM OF CHRISTOPHER GRIEVE (1892–1978)
poet

There is so much that is bad in all the poetry that Scots people know and admire that it is not surprising that for their pet example of a good bad poet they should have to go outside the range of poetry, good, bad, or indifferent altogether. McGonagall is in a very special category, and has it entirely to himself.

Scottish Eccentrics (1936)

CHARLES RENNIE MACKINTOSH
(1868–1928)
architect and designer

———

Don't meddle with other people's ideas when
you have all the work cut out of you in trying
to express your own.

Seemliness (1902)

JOHN MUIR (1838–1914)
naturalist and founder of the
American Natural Park system

Wherever a Scotsman goes, there goes Burns. His grand whole, catholic soul squares with the good of all; therefore we find him in everything everywhere.

John of the Mountains (1938), edited by I. M. Wolfe

MARGARET OLIPHANT (1828–97)
novelist and critic

Life is no definite thing with a beginning and an end, a growth and a climax; but a basket of fragments, passages that lead to nothing, curious incidents which look of importance at first, but which crumble and break into pieces, dropping into ruins.

Review of Henry James's *A London Life* in *Backwoods' Edinburgh Magazine* (1888)

Sir Walter Scott (1771–1832)
novelist and poet

Oh, what a tangled web we weave,
When first we practise to deceive!

Marmion (1808)

I make it a rule to cheat nobody but
booksellers, a race on whom I have no mercy.

Letter to Thomas Sheridan (1811)

To live the life of an author for mere bread is perhaps the most dreadful fate than can be encountered.

Letter to James Bailey (June 1817)

Many a clever boy is flogged into a dunce and many an original composition corrected into mediocrity.

Journal
(June 1826)

But who cares for the whipped cream
of London society?

Journal (April 1828)

Surely chess-playing is a sad waste of brains.

Memoirs of the Life of Walter Scott (1837–8)
by J. G. Lockhart

That terrible Nobody!
How much has he to answer for.
More mischief is done
by Nobody than by
all the world besides.

Thrift (1875)

ADAM SMITH (1723–90)
economist and philosopher

It is not from the benevolence of the butcher, the brewer, or the baker, that we expect our dinner, but from their regard to their own interest.

An Inquiry into the Nature and Causes of the Wealth of Nations (1776)

ALEXANDER SMITH (1829–67)
poet

It is not of so much consequence what you say, as how you say it. Memorable sentences are memorable on account of some single irradiating word.

'On the Writing of Essays', *Dreamthorp* (1863)

TOBIAS SMOLLETT (1721–71)
novelist

London is the devil's drawing-room.

The Adventures of Roderick Random (1748)

Life is no loving father, but a force with
which we must contend and to which we
must adapt the self.

Diary entry (June 1932)

ROBERT LOUIS STEVENSON (1850–94)
novelist, poet and essayist

For my own part, I travel not to go anywhere,
but to go. I travel for travel's sake.

Travels with a Donkey (1879)

From *Virginibus Puerisque* (1881):

Even if we take marriage at its lowest, even if we regard it as no more than a sort of friendship recognized by the police.

You can read Kant by yourself if you wanted, but you must share a joke with someone else. Books are good enough in their own way, but they are a mighty bloodless substitute for life.

It is better to lose health like a spendthrift than to waste it like a miser. It is better to live and be done with it than to die daily in the sick room.

From *Memories and Portraits* (1887):

The first step for all is to learn to the very dregs our own ignoble fallibility.
Faith means holding the same opinions as the person employing the word.

Marriage is one long conversation,
chequered by disputes.

Scientific men, who imagine that their
science affords an answer to the problem of
existence, are perhaps the most to be pitied
of mankind; and contemned.

To travel hopefully is a better thing
than to arrive.

JAMES THOMSON (1700–48)
poet

Poor is the triumph o'er the timid hare!

The Seasons, 'Spring' (1746)

JAMES WATT (1736–1819)
engineer and inventor

I think that I shall not long have anything to
do with the House of Commons again – I
never saw so many wrong-headed people on
all sides gathered together.

Letter to his wife (1767)

Glossary

a' all
ae one
afore before
aft often
agley awry, wrong
ah I
an' and
auld old
bairn child
bane bone
bannock an unleavened cake
bile boil
breid bread
brither brother

bummer a creature that makes a buzzing noise, a bee
canna cannot
canny careful
cauld cold
chiel young man, fellow
claes clothes
cled clad
clout cloth
croon crown
dee die
deil devil
denner dinner

ding deal blows, defeat
dinna don't
doon down
draff pig-food
drap drop
drouth drought, thirst
dunt blow
een eyes
fa' fall
flee fly
fowk folk
frae from
freen friend

fu' full
gab mouth
gae go
gang go
gaun going
gear wealth
gie give
giftie gift
glaikit playful,
    foolish
gree agree
gude good
guid good
ha' haw, hall
hae have
haud hold
hauf half
hause throat
heid head
het hot
i' in
ither other

Janaveer
    January
kail soup; kale
kenna don't
    know
kennin' a little
    bit
kirk church
kitchen relish
lang long
laverock lark
lee lie, to tell
    lies
licht light
lift sky
lo'ed loved
loodest loudest
lowe flame
lowp leap
lug ear
mair more
mak make

maun must
meat food
mennan
    minnow
monie, mony
    many
mou mouth
moyen
    influence
muckle much,
    large
nae no
naething
    nothing
nakit naked
nicht night
no' not
o' of
oot out
parritch
    porridge
pat pot

piece piece of bread, sandwich	**stark** strong	**unca'd** uncalled
pow head	**steekit** closed	**wad** would
rin run	**stoup** flagon, jug	**wame** stomach
shak shake	**tae** to	**wark** work
shoon shoes	**taiken** token	**warld** world
siller silver	**tak** take	**wast** west
skail empty, spill	**thack** thatch	**watter** water
sma' small	**thankit** thanked	**waur** worse
snaw snow	**thigither** together	**weel** well
soo sow	**thoom** thumb	**wersh** tasteless
soor sour	**tint** lost	**whit** what
stamack stomach	**toom** empty	**winna** won't
	tyke dog	**wrang** wrong

IF IT ENDS WELL THEN IT IS WELL